Discussions on the Life of Jesus Christ

Twelve studies
for students
who want to know
more about
the person and
work of Jesus Christ

InterVarsity Press
Downers Grove
Illinois 60515

*Eleventh printing,
December 1977*

*InterVarsity Press is the book
publishing division of
Inter-Varsity Christian
Fellowship, a student
movement active on campus at
hundreds of universities,
colleges and schools of nursing.
For information about
local and regional activities,
write IVCF, 233 Langdon St.,
Madison, WI 53703.*

*Distributed in Canada
through InterVarsity Press,
745 Mount Pleasant Rd.,
Toronto, M4S 2N5.*

ISBN 0-87784-402-X

*Printed in the United
States of America*

contents

introduction

The main purpose of this booklet is to study the basic message of Christianity from the historical record of the Bible. In our society the word "Christian" has many different meanings. For this reason we need to clarify the term by considering the life of Jesus Christ. In so doing, we find ourselves confronted with a living Person, the resurrected Christ, who offers us His personal friendship.

Becoming a Christian is, in a sense, like getting married—it involves a complete committal of one's life to the other person. It demands, therefore, some consideration of basic facts; namely what Christ is like, what claims He makes, and the implications of these claims for our own lives.

The following studies are a guide to several passages where some of these key issues are considered. As the Holy Spirit gives understanding, there will be changed lives because of these studies. Christians will discover more fully the implications of knowing Christ; non-Christians will discover Christ as the source of a new life.

How to Start a Study

1. Pray:
   (a) that specific friends of yours who are not Christians will be interested in studying about the character and teaching of Christ;
   (b) that you will come into contact with people who are questioning the existence of God, the relevance of Christianity, the meaning of life, etc., and that these acquaintances will want to come together for Bible study. Sometimes a Bible study consisting of two persons who are eager to learn is more fruitful than one of ten who come out of duty.

2. Invite:
   (a) After some discussion of Christianity or of life and its problems with your friends, it can be quite natural for you to suggest that you study together the viewpoint of Christ on these issues.
   (b) In addition to inviting friends made in the course of your natural contacts, don't be afraid to go from door to door in the living unit to invite others. You might say politely that you have become interested in Jesus Christ and that you are meeting in your room to discuss with others how knowing Jesus Christ can make a practical difference in your life. Don't give up after issuing such an invitation once around the dorm. Many people have become Christians because someone has consistently and persistently invited them to such studies.

3. Plan:

This Bible study is geared for those who are not Christians. The atmosphere should be one in which they feel free to bring out their problems, doubts, and questions. This cannot be done if Christians outnumber the non-Christians in the study. A good ratio is about six to eight non-Christians to two or three Christians. A larger number of Christians than this could keep many of the people from taking part in the discussion. The two or three Christians in the study should work together closely, while using other Christians to initiate studies of their own, rather than joining the original one.

How to Use This Guide:

1. Leader's Preparation: Before looking at the group discussion questions, read through the Scripture passage and then follow the leader's preparation questions or suggestions. It is important that God speak to you and that you respond personally to the truth revealed before you study it in terms of the group you are going to lead.
2. Possible Approaches: Many times a suitable, questing frame of mind can be created by a realistic introductory question before the group reads the passage. Look over the suggestions and also pray that the Lord will provide you with your own approach adapted to the needs of your particular group.
3. Discussion Questions: These questions are merely suggestions. Work out your own questions in your own words and according to your way of thinking.
4. Additional Questions and Suggestions: These extras are not to be included in the basic study, but are to give an idea of how the basic study can be expanded. Because of limited time and background, some groups will find the basic questions adequate.

a friend of social outcasts

Passage: Luke 18:35—19:10.

Purpose: To show Christ's attitude toward the needy; i.e. He is interested in those with real needs, no matter who they are, and by His actions He shows love for them.

Leader's Preparation:

1. Read through the passage twice, asking God to guide your thinking and understanding.
2. List all the people (individuals and groups) in the passage and note their reactions to each other.
3. Compare Jesus and the crowd in relation to (a) their attitude toward the blind man, (b) their attitude toward Zacchaeus, (c) the action taken in both cases.
4. Examine yourself as to your (a) awareness of the needs of individuals around you, (b) your attitude toward needy people who are socially "unacceptable," (c) the action you take toward them. Are you more like Jesus Christ or more like the crowd?
5. What were the results of each incident—for (a) the blind man, (b) Zacchaeus?
6. In what ways does Jesus Christ meet your needs and change your life?

Introducing the Passage:

(a) Luke 18:35—43: Have everyone read this passage silently, then have someone tell the story to the rest

of the group as if he were actually there. Now use the first set of discussion questions.
(b) Luke 19:1—10: Have one person read the story of Zacchaeus aloud to the group, using a modern translation. Before you begin with the discussion questions on this section, explain why publicans were hated by the Jews. (Publicans were Jews who collected taxes for the Romans and who often collected exorbitant and unfair amounts of taxes from their own people.) Note that Zacchaeus was the chief publican.

Discussion Questions for Luke 18:35—43:

1. How was the blind man brought into contact with Jesus? How much initiative was there on the beggar's part? How much initiative on Jesus' part?
2. What attitude did the crowd have toward the blind man?
3. What were the results of this meeting (a) for the blind man, (b) for the crowd, (c) for Christ?
4. What do you think was Christ's attitude toward the unwanted beggar? Why did He bother with him?

Discussion Questions for Luke 19:1—10:

1. Contrast Zacchaeus with the blind man in (a) their social standing, and (b) their sense of need.
2. How was Zacchaeus brought into contact with Jesus? How much initiative was there on Zacchaeus' part? How much initiative on Jesus' part? How did this differ from the meeting of the beggar?
3. What did the crowd feel Jesus' reaction to Zacchaeus should be?
4. Why did Jesus invite himself to go *home* with Zacchaeus? (Remember the Jews' attitude toward publicans.)
5. How did Jesus' attitude toward these two men differ from the attitude of the crowd? If these events occurred today, do you think the crowd would act any differently?

6. Why do you think Christ wanted to associate with men like the blind beggar and Zacchaeus at the risk of His reputation?

Additional Questions and Suggestions:

1. What is the relationship between Christ's concern and action in meeting the specific physical and social needs of men and in His meeting their basic spiritual need?
2. What reasons motivate us to examine the life of Jesus Christ? What needs do we have? What needs in our lives does He meet?
3. Make a list of all the characteristics of Jesus Christ you can find in this passage.

an upsetting dinner party

Passage: Luke 7:36—50.

Purpose: To show Christ's attitude toward sinners, His love for them, His willingness to forgive them on the basis not of who they are but of their faith in Him.

Background Material: During the time that Christ lived here on earth, sandals were removed at meals, and guests reclined on their elbows with their feet stretched out behind them. Starting with verse 44, Jesus mentions three acts of courtesy with which a host usually received an honored guest: he washed the guest's feet at the door (sandals were scant protection against dusty roads), greeted the guest with a kiss (like a handshake today), and anointed his head with oil (used to point out a chief guest, as does seating a person on the right of the host or hostess). The woman performed all three of these courtesies, which Simon should have extended. Make sure that the group understands what a Pharisee was, namely, a religious leader who prided himself on the strict observance of the law and who in general was highly self-righteous.

Leader's Preparation:

1. Read through the passage, listing the people mentioned and noting their reactions to one another.

2. Pray for insight and understanding as you study this passage.
3. Consider the woman and Simon, noting (a) their attitudes toward themselves, (b) their attitudes toward Jesus, (c) how they were influenced by social pressure.
4. How did Jesus treat each of them?
5. Put yourself in the place of (a) Jesus, (b) the woman, (c) Simon. Ask yourself: (1) How am I like this person? (2) How am I different from this person? (3) In what ways do I need to be changed?

Possible Approaches:

1. Discuss how you feel when you are not completely accepted by the people you are with. Encourage the group to look for Jesus' attitude and action in the strained social situation in this passage.
2. How much do one's associations influence the type of reputation he has? (Is good company a criterion for respectability?). Encourage the group to look for the opinions on the subject in this passage. Read the passage out loud in a modern translation.

Discussion Questions:

1. Why do you suppose Simon invited Christ to dinner? What leads us to believe that He was not completely welcome?
2. Why do you think Christ accepted the invitation?
3. What was this woman's attitude toward Christ? How was it expressed in what she did to Him?
4. Why did Jesus let the disturbance go on? Why didn't He ask her to leave and meet Him at a more convenient time?
5. What upset Simon?
6. What did he mean by "sinner" (see verse 39—a woman of low morals)?
7. How did Jesus show Simon, the Pharisee, that it was not ignorance that made Christ allow this woman to touch Him?

8. Have someone retell the parable in his own words. What is the main point of the parable?
9. How did Christ's attitude toward the woman differ from Simon's? Would most people today have the attitude of Christ or Simon toward such a woman?
10. Compare the attitude and action of the woman toward Christ with Simon's attitude and action toward Christ.
11. What was the reaction of the other guests to the situation?
12. In summary describe Christ's attitude toward sinners like Simon and the woman.

Additional Questions and Suggestions:

1. In what ways in our society today does the stigma attached to personal association with social "outcasts" keep us from helping to meet the needs of such people?
2. What motivates us to love Jesus Christ? How is this love demonstrated to an unseen Person?
3. What do we mean by the word sinner? How are we made aware of our own sin? Is Jesus intimating in this passage that there are degrees of sin?
4. List all the characteristics of Jesus Christ that you can find in the passage.

Christ's diagnosis of man

Passage: Mark 7:1—23.

Purpose: To consider Christ's definition of sin, and His exposure of those who follow the traditions of men rather than God's Word.

Background Material: The Pharisees and scribes were the religious leaders of Jesus' day. Very often He condemned them for their hypocrisy, as He does in this passage. (See Luke 11:39 and 12:1.) The Pharisee's emphasis on washing hands was not for hygienic purposes but to cleanse himself from accidental contact with people or things less righteous than he. He distinguished also between clean and unclean meat, etc. Note how Jesus declares all clean in verse 19. A practice of religious Jews was to pledge money for the temple treasury and defer payment until after death. A man then could tell his parents, when they were needy, that he had no money to help them because it was "Corban," meaning "dedicated under oath." In this way a "religious" tradition was used as an escape from obeying a very clear command of God. It is true that Jesus does not here use the word "sin," but he very clearly speaks of disobedience to God, of defilement, and in verses 21-22 he lists a number of "sins." His topic is clearly sin.

Leader's Preparation:

1. Pray that God will clearly show you His view of sin.
2. Read the passage noting the main emphasis of the Pharisees. How does Jesus differ from them?
3. Read Matt. 22:37—40. Study the specific sins listed by Christ in Mark 7, and note how each one is related to the two great commandemnts.
4. Examine yourself with reference to each of the sins mentioned. How does your evaluation differ if you include inward motivation as well as outward behavior?
5. After the above study, how would you define sin?

Possible Approaches:

1. In our previous study Jesus talked about sin and sinners. Look for his meaning of what sin is as you read Mark 7.
2. If someone uses the word *sin*, what do you think of? In Mark 7, we have two different ideas of sin. Look for them as you read.

Discussion Questions:

1. What action of Jesus' disciples did the scribes and Pharisees criticize?
2. Why did the Pharisees and scribes think that this issue was important?
3. What did Jesus say was wrong with their attitude (6-8)?
4. What specific command of God had been disobeyed by the scribes and Pharisees? What do you think had caused a tradition of men to pervert a commandment of God? (See background material.)
5. How does Jesus summarize the commandments of God? See Matt. 22:37—40.
6. Does this command deal with overt behavior or inward motivation and desires? Where does it place the emphasis? Where did the Pharisees place the emphasis?

7. Why were men's traditions so important to the Pharisees?
8. From this passage, how would the Pharisees define sin? How did Jesus define sin?
9. Read through the specific sins that are listed by Christ. Discuss how each one breaks one or both of the two great commandments. What distinction does Christ make between major and minor sins?
10. Summarize Jesus' view of the source of sin.
11. Can we overcome sin by disciplining or controlling our outward behavior? If not, what can we do about our condition?

Additional Questions and Suggestions:

1. Today in many circles, sin is considered relative. How does this viewpoint compare with Jesus' teaching?
2. Can a person love God without loving his neighbor or loving himself? What is the relationship?
3. List all the characteristics of Jesus Christ that you find in this passage.

purpose and destiny in life

Passage: John 8:12—47.

Purpose: To see the uniqueness of Jesus Christ in His origin, His self-knowledge, His divine destiny, and His relationship to the Father.

Leader's Preparation:

1. Pray for a clear understanding of the passage as it relates to you and the others in your Bible study group.
2. Read the passage to find out the significance of Jesus' description of Himself as the Light of the world.
3. What reasons did Jesus give the Jews for believing in Him?
4. Contrast Jesus and the Jews with regard to (a) their origin, (b) their destiny, (c) their relationship to God.
5. What is the result of believing that Jesus Christ is the light of the world? What difference has it made in your life?

Possible Approaches:

1. Discuss the function of light.
2. Read this passage to see how Jesus describes Himself as the Light.

Discussion Questions:

1. How did the Pharisees respond to Jesus' claim to

be the Light of the world?
2. What facts did Jesus give to authenticate His claims?
3. Why did Jesus say they could not come where He was going?
4. Did they get the point?
5. What did Jesus tell them of (a) their origin, (b) their destiny, (c) their way of escape?
6. How did Jesus identify Himself?
7. What was the response?
8. What did Jesus expect from a follower besides belief in His person (v. 31)?
9. What do you think He meant by "continue in my word"? What does this kind of belief lead to (v. 32)? How did the Jews who possessed only an intellectual belief respond?
10. Who is enslaved by sin? Can the non-Christian enjoy true freedom?
11. What indications are there in this passage that Jesus' origin was different from His hearers'?
12. Light exposes things as they really are. It also gives direction. How did Jesus enlighten the Jews in regard to (a) themselves, (b) Himself?
13. What direction did He give to them?
14. If one responds to Jesus Christ as the Light, how does this affect one's (a) origin, (b) present state, (c) destiny?

Additional Questions and Suggestions:

1. How does Jesus Christ affect our understanding of ourselves and our destiny? How does He help us to see things as they really are? What misconceptions do we share with the Jews?
2. What is the ultimate source of human freedom? How can we *know* the truth? How can we know liberty?
3. List all the characteristics of Jesus Christ that you find in this passage.

the identity of Jesus Christ

Passage: Luke 5:17—26.

Purpose: To find out who Jesus Christ is.

Background Material: This may be helpful if it is brought in briefly at the appropriate place in the discussion.

(1) *Palsy,* the disease that the man had, is a type of paralysis. This will already be clear if modern versions are used.

(2) The Pharisees and scribes, who had come from "every town of Galilee, and Judea, and Jerusalem" (Luke 5:17), had come a distance of 75 miles or more.

(3) The Scribes were keepers and interpreters of the Old Scriptures, experts in both civil and religious matters. The Pharisees were a class of people who devoted themselves to a rigid observance of the laws of their religion. For a more complete explanation, see note 1, page 241, of Phillips' *The Gospels.*

Leader's Preparation:

1. Pray that you will clearly understand the significance of the claims Jesus makes in this passage.
2. As you read, note all the persons mentioned and their reactions to each other.
3. What is the answer to Jesus' question in verse 23?

4. List all the characteristics of Jesus Christ you can find in this passage in regard to (a) His opinion of Himself, (b) His understanding of people, (c) His power.

Possible Approaches:

1. The fascination of being in a place where there is a crowd of people often comes from the variety of reactions of individuals to each other and to the focus of attention. In Luke 5 Jesus is in a crowded home. As you read what happened, note the various emotions and reactions.
2. Read the passage aloud in one or two versions (RSV, Williams, Phillips, etc.).
3. For the purpose of familiarizing each person with the passage, summarize each major action in a series of three-word statements. Jesus teaches crowd, men bring paralytic, crowd blocks door, etc. This can best be done by having a few minutes in which each person can draw up his own list; then have two or three lists read to the group.

Discussion Questions:

1. How eager were the men to get to Jesus with their sick friend? What might have stirred them to this unusual act of ripping a hole in the roof to get to Christ?
2. What is the first recorded reaction of the scribes and Pharisees? Why did they object to Jesus' words? Did Jesus disagree with their implied assertion that only God can forgive sin?
3. Compare Jesus' attitude with that of the scribes and Pharisees toward the sick man and his friends. If this incident occurred on this campus, do you think the attitude of the scribes and Pharisees might be found today?
4. How is Jesus' evaluation of Himself different from that of the scribes and Pharisees? Why do you suppose

they would not accept what He said about Himself?

5. Discuss the issue in verse 23 from the standpoint of human possibility, then from that of God's ability. According to verses 24 and 25, what did the issue mean to Jesus?

6. To sum up, discuss (a) what different people in the passage thought about Christ, (b) what He revealed about Himself.

Additional Questions and Suggestions:

1. What is the relationship of Jesus' miracles to His teaching? Is Jesus concerned only with man's spiritual welfare?

2. What made it difficult for the Jews to believe that Jesus is God? What reasons did Jesus give them for believing? How could the Jews explain Jesus' words and works if they did not accept Him as God? On college campuses today, do you find similar situations caused by disbelief—in spite of evidence that cannot be explained apart from belief in the God-Man, Christ Jesus?

humanitarianism according to Jesus

Passage: Luke 18:18—30.

Purpose: To show that religious activity is insufficient for eternal life.

Leader's Preparation:

1. Ask God to guide your thinking and understanding as you read this passage.
2. List all you learn about (a) the rich young ruler, (b) Christ.
3. How can this passage personally affect your thinking and action?

Possible Approaches:

1. If someone asked you how to inherit eternal life, what would you say? In this passage, a young man asks Jesus this question; note what His answer is.
2. Is it possible to regard Jesus just as a good teacher? In the passage you are going to read, a young man comes to Jesus. Try to find out what he thought of Jesus.

Discussion Questions:

1. Why did this young man come to Jesus? Why did he feel Jesus would help him?

2. Why did Jesus parry the question at first? Why was He drawing attention to Himself? Was He saying He did not deserve the title "good"?
3. What authority did Jesus use in answering this man's question? Did He include all the Ten Commandments? Which part of the Ten Commandments did He select as His basis for communication with His inquirer?
4. How did the young man evaluate himself? Was he proud, deceived, or able honestly to appraise himself?
5. Specifically what did Jesus say he needed to do? (Note two actions or series of actions.) Would God necessarily exact the same requirement of everyone seeking eternal life? What is Jesus really asking?
6. What does the young ruler's response indicate about his attitude toward (a) himself, (b) Jesus Christ, (c) his fellow-men?
7. Why did Jesus make discipleship so difficult for this eager, rich young man whose support might have been a great help to His cause?
8. What do we learn about Jesus Christ from this passage?
9. Can we believe in Jesus Christ as a good teacher but not as God himself?
10. This passage causes us to ask: What is our attitude toward eternal life? toward ourselves? our fellow-men? Jesus Christ?

Additional Questions and Suggestions:

1. If Jesus is not God, is He a good teacher? Why?
2. Compare this passage with Luke 10:25—37 as to (a) motivation of questioner, (b) answer of Jesus, (c) authority used, (d) results (if mentioned).
3. List all the characteristics of Jesus Christ that you can find in this passage.

is Jesus the answer to life?

Passage: John 14.

Purpose: To realize that if we are to know God and Life, in this world and the next, Jesus Christ is indispensable.

Leader's Preparation:

1. Pray that through this study God the Holy Spirit will deepen your realization of who Jesus Christ is.
2. List all the people in this passage; what do you find out about each one?
3. List all the claims Jesus makes for Himself. What is the significance of each claim for your life?

Possible Approaches:

1. Discuss how you feel when you make a definite statement, only to have someone ask a question already answered in your preceding remark. This happened in today's passage. Look for the reactions as you read.
2. Discuss essential (non-physical) needs of people today e.g., for direction, motivation, strength, a sense of destiny, truth. Consider their pre-eminent need for

the knowledge of Christ and the presence of God with them. In this passage Jesus talks about some of these subjects. Look for them as you read.
3. Note the questions and requests of the disciples as Jesus talks with them in John 14:1—11.

Discussion Questions:

1. In this passage we read of two disciples of Jesus, Thomas and Philip. What was the interest of each?
2. How did Jesus answer Thomas?
3. What difference would it make if Jesus had said, "I will show you the way, I will tell you the truth, and I will give you life," rather than what He did say? Why did Jesus seem to direct people to His own person and not just to His teachings?
4. What was Philip's request?
5. How does Christ answer him?
6. How does this answer compare to the answer Christ gave Thomas? What is the relationship between finding direction, truth and life, and finding God Himself?
7. Was Christ claiming to be just a godly man or a Man who was God? On what Scripture do you base your answer?
8. What relationship did Jesus claim to have to the Father?
9. Why did He expect Philip and the other disciples to believe Him?
10. What did He mean when He said, "I am the Way"? What did He mean when He said, "I am the Truth"? Can any truth be considered as fundamentally separable from Him who *is* Truth?
11. What is the meaning of "I am the Life"? If He is Life, if Life is in Him, can we live apart from Him?
12. How is the relationship between the Father and Son (v. 10) similar to the relationship Christ wants with us? See v. 28.
13. If Jesus is who He says He is, and we come into

a basic personal relationship with Him, how will our lives be affected?

14. Is it possible to be acquainted with the life of Christ and His teaching and not really know Him? Why?

Additional Questions and Suggestions:

1. In discussing the relationship of Jesus Christ (who is God the Son) to God the Father, the doctrine of the Trinity arises. This tremendous truth will never be fully understood on earth by finite minds. But we are confronted with these facts: first, that "the Lord our God is one God," and second, that three Persons have the attributes of deity: God the Father, Jesus Christ, and the Holy Spirit. Therefore, we conclude with historic Christianity that there is a unity of Being but three distinct Persons, co-existent, co-equal, one in three, three in one. How this can be, we do not comprehend. However, we accept the facts which the Bible clearly states, and ask God to show us what He would of their significance for us. For instance, we derive our concept of personality from the Godhead. Yet we may also realize from the Godhead that the end of personality is not individuality, but oneness. As Christ was one with His Father, we are to be one with Him and with each other in Him. There can be no oneness when there is only one; two or more are needed for oneness.

2. In this passage Jesus continually pointed to His own person as the source of life and truth. He indicated that joining ourselves to Him would supply the closeness to God, the knowledge and power in life that we need. How does this teaching make Christ different from other religious teachers?

the crucifixion of Christ

Passage: Luke 23:26—56

Purpose: To consider the events at the crucifixion of the Lord Jesus Christ, particularly as recorded in verses 33—49.

Background Material: This study concentrates on facts surrounding Christ's crucifixion; the why of His death will be considered specifically in our next study.

This is not to suggest, however, a casual or impersonal approach to these stupendous events. As we seek to understand this portion of Scripture, we remember that it was God's Anointed, His Chosen, the Fellow of the Lord of hosts (Zech. 13:7) who in a body of flesh and blood like ours lived, suffered, and died—the shameful public death of a criminal. This Man who was ridiculed, abused, and tormented was the Lion of the tribe of Judah (Rev. 5:5), the Image of the invisible God (Col. 1:15),—and the Lamb of God who takes away the sin of the world (John 1:29).

Leader's Preparation:

1. Read and reread this passage, with an undivided and undistracted mind. Live with it until it lays hold on you.

2. Read the accounts of the crucifixion in the other Gospels and in Psalms 22 and 69.
3. The Spirit of God inspired detailed descriptions of the crucifixion in psalms written many hundreds of years before that event took place. Ask Him to illumine the written Word of God now for you, and for the sake of those in your study group.

Possible Approaches:

1. Have each member of the group read the passage silently. Then ask someone to tell the story of the crucifixion as if he had been one of the eye-witnesses.
2. Assign the roles of the passage's individuals or groups to members of the study group. Also choose a narrator and read the passage in this way.

Discussion Questions:

1. What was Jesus' first cry from the cross? What does it reveal about Christ, even in the midst of great suffering?
2. The first three hours of the crucifixion were full of activity. What was taking place at the feet of the Crucified (v. 34)?
3. What were the actions of those gathered at Golgotha (v. 35)?
4. What would you expect to be the dominant emotion of people "who stood looking on"—genuine concern or stolid indifference? Do you consider this attitude toward Christ at all typical of the world today, of your own campus?
5. Why did the rulers (the religious leaders) hate the Lord so intensely? Did they have any place in their religion for a divine and crucified Christ? Does this situation pertain anywhere today?
6. Three times Christ was challenged to save Himself as He had saved others. Had He accepted the challenge, what would have happened (a) to His relationship of perfect obedience to the Father, (b) to His word, and (c) to us?

7. What response did Jesus make to the derision of the rulers, the soldiers, and the railing thiefs. What does this indicate to you about His character?
8. Did He respond with silence to the other thief's cry for mercy? What do you think brought this robber to penitence and faith—a faith that is rather remarkable considering the surroundings? Did Jesus give him what he asked—or more than that in His assurance of full salvation? How could Jesus offer this salvation to a criminal so freely?
9. Although God did not intervene to spare His Son the suffering of the cross, what evidence can you find in this passage that God was at work at Calvary?

Suggested break for a second discussion.

10. What occurred at the sixth hour (noon)? What is indicated by the statement that "the sun was darkened" or "the sun's light failed"? Since the darkness lasted three hours, and the longest eclipse can last but a few minutes, can this event be considered an ordinary eclipse? Consider also that the crucifixion occurred during the festival of the Passover, which was always observed at the time of the full moon when an eclipse of the sun is impossible.
11. You will note from this passage that the three hours of extraordinary darkness, as the Light of the world was dying, were strangely silent ones. Luke records no activity from the sixth to the ninth hour. Do you think that darkness served to shut Him off from witnesses of His anguish which will always be to us inconceivable? What else may the darkness have symbolized or signified?
12. What is the meaning of the rending of the veil of the temple? The veil was a curtain that concealed the Holy of Holies, where no man could enter except the high priest, bearing the blood of the atonement and the smoke of incense—and that only once a year. Note that the rending of this veil in the middle

(v. 45), in two pieces, from the top to the bottom (Mt. 27:51) coincided with the Lord's death. The hour was three o'clock, the time of the beginning of the evening sacrifice, so that the priests were then in the temple at their duties before the veil when this event took place.

13. Look up Hebrews 10:18—22. What do these verses tell you of the significance of the rending of the temple veil?

14. Observe that Jesus cried "with a loud voice" immediately before He died. Is this shout of victory what you would naturally expect to hear from a man exhausted by indescribable spiritual suffering and the agonies of death by crucifixion?

15. What is the significance of the statement, "He gave up the ghost" (v. 46, KJV)? Some modern translators say here, "He died"; but all the evangelists seem deliberately to avoid this expression. The Greek words they use imply an act of will and mean: He gave His life away. His death was voluntary in the absolute sense of the term. Compare John 10:17, 18.

16. Mark 15:39 tells us that when the centurion saw that Jesus "so cried out, and gave up the ghost, he said, 'Truly this man was the Son of God.'" Can you explain why?

17. How do you account for the change in the attitude of the people from verse 35 to verse 48? What were they feeling now? Is it likely that they understood the full significance of the death of Christ, since His own disciples did not? How much did they realize, do you think?

18. As you consider now the Lord's death, do you feel that the extraordinary events that accompanied it showed the unique and supernatural character of that death? Viewing it in retrospect, do you agree with the centurion: "Truly this man was the Son of God"?

why did Christ die?

Passage: Isaiah 52:13—53:12

Purpose: To realize the vital importance to us of Christ's death; to understand that its value is personal, decisive, abiding, and eternal.

Background Material: In our last study, we looked at some of the events through which God authenticated and interpreted the death of His Son. We saw that, following these events, the crowds beat their breasts, in part fulfilling Zechariah 12:10: "... they shall look upon me whom they have pierced, and they shall mourn for him, as one mourneth for his only son, and shall be in bitterness for him, as one that is in bitterness for his firstborn."

Like the Roman centurion and the repentant thief, these people realized at last that Jesus was innocent, righteous, divine. They must have sensed at least their own guilt in His crucifixion.

Was the death of Jesus a tragic mistake, some fateful miscarriage of human justice? Why did Christ die?

The death of Christ is the dominant message of the Christian faith. To be understood, it must be seen to embrace other central biblical truths. One truth is that of man's estrangement from God through sin; man's enmity toward His Creator; man's rebellion against the Lord of the universe. If sin is viewed as religious fiction instead of death-producing fact, the Cross becomes irrelevant. God's hatred of sin, His consuming holiness, and His justice—which makes it impossible for sin to go unpunished—all God's attributes including His incredible love meet at the cross of Christ. There God in Christ offered Himself in love for us, as the perfect sacrifice and satisfaction that the justice of God demanded.

Leader's Preparation:

1. Pray for yourself that God may give you a new comprehension of the Cross and its meaning for you.
2. Go through this study carefully, looking up all the Scripture references included and reading them thoughtfully and prayerfully.
3. Ask the Lord to help you share His truth with others. Pray for the individuals in your group, especially for those who may not know the love and power of Jesus Christ in their own lives.
4. As you consider Jesus who is "the propitiation for our sins: and not for ours only, but also for the sins of the whole world," pray that the implications of I John 2:2 may be real to every member of the group.

NOTE: This study may well require more than one study period. Take time to prepare and conduct it. The subject is too big and too important to be rushed.

Possible Approaches:

1. Ask the group to read the Isaiah passage silently.
2. Have two people participate in reading these verses aloud. (Ask them as far ahead as possible, so that they will have time to prepare and read intelligently.) Since God and man, reconciled, share the telling here, ask the first person to read Isaiah

52:13—15 the second Isaiah 53:1—10 with the first person returning to read Isaiah 53:11, 12.

Discussion Questions:

1. In Luke's account of the crucifixion which we read last time, a number of details foretold by Isaiah in the verses we have just read were literally fulfilled. Can you point out these prophecies?
2. From what verses in Isaiah 53 can we assert that Jesus' death was neither unexpected nor accidental?
3. Ask the group to turn to Acts 2:22, 23. How do the roles of God and man meet in Jesus' death? Compare Luke 22:22.
4. Note Isaiah 53:10: "Yet it pleased the Lord to bruise (Heb. pierce) him." That the Cross was part of God's eternal purpose may be seen in John's reference to Jesus as "the Lamb slain from the foundation of the world" (Rev. 13:8). But did the Man Christ Jesus know that the end of His earthly ministry was to be violent death? See John 3:14; 8:28; Mark 10:32—34, 45.
5. Was Christ more than the passive, obedient servant foretold in Isaiah 53? Was He also the willing actor, choosing the costly path that reconciled us to God? Ask individuals in the group to read aloud Psalm 40:7, 8; Isaiah 50:6; Hebrews 12:2.

NOTE: It is important here to remember that Jesus Christ is not a third party, coming between a holy God and sinful men. He is God Himself, who paid the price of sin. He is also Man, who identified Himself with sinful men, putting Himself in our place, and experiencing for us a death that was rightfully ours, not His.

As the unique God-Man, he can represent both sides, and He alone can do so. That is why there is "one mediator between God and men, the man Christ Jesus" (1 Timothy 2:5). There is no other. He is alone. He is sufficient.

6. Read Romans 5:8 and ask someone else to look up 1 Corinthians 15:3. For whom and for what does the Apostle Paul say Christ died?
7. Link these simple four- and five-word statements—"Christ died for us" and "Christ died for our sins"—with parallel passages in Isaiah 53. Do apostle and prophet agree?
8. Do you find a parallel between the change in reaction of the crowd at the crucifixion reported by Luke and the development in understanding of the "we" of Isaiah? Note in the latter's account that at first many were astonished at the strange suffering and concluded that the Sufferer was smitten of God (as though for His own sin). Then comes the realization of His sinlessness and of their own implication in His death.
9. In Isaiah 53:6, how does God define the iniquity that necessitated His death? What is the inevitable end of all sin or iniquity? See Romans 6:23.
10. If God had not made Jesus the sin offering, could many have been justified (vs. 10, 11)? Would the Lord have seen His seed (His spiritual offspring, the redeemed of God) or the travail of His soul and been satisfied? What does the "therefore" of verse 12 follow and rest upon? Note also the "because" of verse 12 and the clauses it introduces. What do you conclude from this?

Suggested break for a second discussion.

11. Read aloud II Corinthians 5:21. Describe in your own words the complete exchange God effected through the Cross. Can you explain the statement in Ephesians 1:6: "he hath made us accepted in the beloved"?
12. Have someone read Colossians 1:21, 22. Would you say from verse 22 that God's will is to make us not only accepted, but acceptable? Whom are we to be like? See Romans 8:29.

13. The offering of the body of Jesus Christ once for all, as one sacrifice for sins for ever (Hebrews 10; 10, 12) has many specific consequences. Included among them are those referred to in the following Scriptures. Read and consider each group separately.

I John 1:7—2:2	The power of Christ's saving death is present and continuing.
Hebrews 9:12–14	Our deliverance is eternal, and enables us to serve the living God.
Ephesians 2:8–10	We are God's handiwork, created to perform the good works He has planned for us.
Ephesians 5:1, 2 Romans 12:1, 2 I John 3:16	Our life is to be one of love, as was His. This love involves sacrifice—to God... ... and for men.
Revelation 12:11	The victory of God's servants is irrevocably bound to His death.
Colossians 1:19, 20	The scope of Christ's reconciling death extends beyond the world of men to all creation.

14. According to the Bible, Christ's death was for His people Israel, for the Gentiles, for all, for all nations, for the whole world. Are the benefits of His sacrifice available to anyone at all? See John 3:16.

15. The Bible also tells us (Matt. 26:26—28; Luke 22: 19, 20; I Cor. 11:23—26) that the same night in which He was betrayed, the Lord Jesus took bread, and when He had given thanks, He brake it, and said, "Take, eat: this is My Body, which is broken for you." Why was the bread broken (and the wine poured out)?

What did the broken bread symbolize? Compare John 6:33—35. What must the Bread of God do with His life to be able to satisfy forever the hunger of man?

16. Why do you think that Jesus, in giving the broken bread to His disciples, commanded, "Take, eat"?

17. Have someone read Galatians 2:20. Can the true believer be divorced from Christ in His death and life? On what personal ground does Paul base his identification with the Son of God?

18. Is life in Chirst forced upon us? Are the benefits of the atonement (the at-one-ment or reconcilation of God and man) universally and inescapably ours? Or is something required of us? See Isaiah 55:6—9 and Romans 2:4.

19. Can forgiveness be had apart from the Forgiver—life apart from the God who is Life? Have someone read I John 5:11, 12. Then read aloud and compare John 3:36.

20. The doctrine of the atonement is often summarized in the words: "By grace, for Christ's sake, by faith." On the basis of this study, can you explain these words? Read Romans 5:1, 6—11. Close with the reading of Ephesians 2:4—10.

the resurrection of Christ

Passage: Luke 24.

Purpose: To consider some of the historic evidence of the Lord Jesus Christ's resurrection from the dead.

Background Material: The resurrection of Jesus Christ is more than a narrative, more than a symbol. It is the completion and evidence of what may be considered an even greater miracle: the fact that Christ died for our sins to bring us to God. It is the proof of the Atonement, of God's acceptance of Christ's sacrifice of Himself, as He took our place in death that we might share His place in life.

"This Jesus," Peter declared before thousands of people who had known of Christ, in the city outside which He had died only a few weeks before—that is, where and when the facts were easily verifiable—"This Jesus God raised up, and of that we all are witnesses (Acts 2:32)."

The New Testament knows none other than a living Savior. Its gospel has no ultimate meaning apart from the empty tomb. For He was the Life that death could not hold (Acts 2:24). He was "designated Son of God in power according to the Spirit of holiness by his resurrection from the dead..." (Rom. 1:4).

Leader's Preparation:

1. Read and reread prayerfully, not only Luke 24, but also the parallel passages in the other gospels (Matt. 28, Mark 16, John 20).
2. As you read these Scriptures, put yourself in the place of the grieving women at the tomb and of Christ's dejected, defeated disciples. Remember, they did not yet understand Jesus' teaching that He would rise from the dead, so try to comprehend their predisposition *not* to believe in this miracle. What do they experience as they finally realize that their Lord lives?
3. Pray that the fact of the empty tomb and a risen, living Savior may be increasingly real to you. Ask that those who study with you may share in the truth and joy of the Lord's resurrection.

Possible Approaches:

1. Well ahead of time, ask five people in the group to be prepared to read designated sections of this long chapter aloud.
2. A suggested division is as follows: verses 1—12; 13—24; 25—35; 36—43; 44—53. Have these passages read before the appropriate questions on them as indicated in the text, rather than all at once at the beginning of the study.
3. It will probably be wise to devote at least two sessions to this study, beginning the second session perhaps with question 10.

Discussion Questions:

1. Luke 24:1—12. When the women came to the tomb early on what was destined to be the first Christian Sunday, what were they expecting to find? Is a dead Christ the object of our adoration?
2. What did the angels' question help the women to understand? Are we ever frustrated in our spiritual searching because we are looking for the wrong thing?

Do we try to limit God's activity by our own expectations?

3. What were the women asked to remember? Is there a connection in verses 8 and 9 between Jesus' words remembered, or the Word of God, and the women's dawning belief? Compare John 2:22.

Beginning with this incident, note in the resurrection narratives how differently the Lord deals with individuals as He brings them to more complete faith in Himself. List the means.

4. Have someone read John 20:11—16. What do you think was the purpose of the questions which the angels and then Jesus put to Mary Magdalene? At what point did Mary recognize her Lord? Compare John 10:3 and 27. What does Mark 16:9 tell us of Mary Magdalene's previous experience with Christ? What possible significance do you find in the fact that, after His resurrection, He appeared first of all to her? What does this indicate to you about the Lord?

5. Note Luke 24:9—11. Were the disciples eager or reluctant to accept this report of the resurrection? Could you describe them as possessing "the will to believe"? Various versions of verse 11 describe the women's words as seeming to the apostles "idle talk," "sheer imagination," "nonsense," "rubbish"—and "they would not believe them."

6. What actions of Peter are recorded in verse 12? What significance is there in the fact of the linen clothes that had wrapped the dead body of Jesus lying by themselves? If friends or enemies had been willing and able to steal the body of Jesus in spite of the heavy Roman guard before the tomb, where would the grave clothes have been? At the sight of the empty tomb and the arrangement of the burial linens, did Peter believe or wonder? What more did Peter evidently require? See Luke 24:34; I Corinthians 15:5.

7. Have someone read the parallel passage in John

20:1—8. What is the significance of the detailed description of the grave clothes in verse 7? Is there an indication here that they had not been touched by human hands? In verse 8, what result did this evidence have on John, the disciple who was closest to Jesus?

8. Ask a member of the group to read Matthew 28:11—15. Is the theory that the disciples stole the body of Jesus plausible? Aside from the evidence contained in these verses, is such a theory psychologically or ethically defensible considering the apostles' state at the time and their later triumphant witness, come life or death?

9. A related theory is recorded in John 20:2: Mary Magdalene at first concluded that the authorities or enemies of Jesus had taken His body from the tomb. If they had done so, would the scene recorded in Matthew 28:11—15 have taken place? All the authorities had to do to nip the troublesome resurrection "heresy" in the bud was to produce the body of Jesus!

Suggested break for a second discussion.

10. Have two people read Luke 24:13—24 and 25—35. Note that Luke the physician was an extraordinarily accurate historian. Take time to observe the style of this and other biblical accounts of resurrection events. What does their detail and dignity and restraint suggest to you? If you had been making up this story, would you have had the Lord appear first to Mary Magdalene, or do you think you would have given this honor to His mother Mary or to one of the "important" disciples? Would you have omitted through reticence the account of Christ's meeting with Peter, the disciple who had vehemently betrayed Him? What do such considerations contribute to your recognition of the authenticity of the biblical records?

11. In Luke 24:25, how does the Lord (still unrecognized) describe the response of Cleopas and his com-

panion to the resurrection? What should they have been quick to believe? To what does He refer them —an event, an experience, or the written Word of God? According to Christ's own testimony, does the Old Testament set forth Jesus? See verses 27 and 44.

12. Have Luke 24:36—43 read. Did the disciples believe the witness of the Emmaus disciples any more than they had believed the women's report? What was their reaction in verse 37 to Jesus' presence among them? What proofs of His identity did their Lord offer them? What was the progression of their emotions and conviction recorded here?

13. Luke 24:44—53. Contrast the state of the apostles after Christ's ascension (verses 52 and 53) and early on the resurrection day. Did they feel that they had lost Him again, as they had thought they had lost Him once in death? Describe in your own words what had happened to them.

14. Note verse 48. What are the disciples, according to their Lord? What does "these things" refer to? Compare Acts 1:21, 22; 2:32 and I Corinthians 15:1—8.

15. In preceding studies on the crucifixion and its meaning, we considered the fact that "Christ died for our sins in accordance with the scriptures." In I Corinthians 15:3, 4, Paul speaks of two other facts as being "of first importance." What are they?

16. Review the evidence—the testimony of unbelieving Jews and Romans, and of slow-believing disciples, considered in this study—that a dead Christ was buried in a tomb that was subsequently found empty. Consider that the Church was born in an area and time where these facts were public knowledge. "This thing was not done in a corner," Paul said (Acts 26:26).

17. Review the appearances of the risen Christ considered in this study—to Mary Magdalene, the two Emmaus disciples, to Peter, to the larger group of disciples, to "more than five hundred brethren at one

time," and to James, the unsympathetic brother of Jesus who later became the leader of the Jerusalem church and witnessed to his natural brother as "our Lord Jesus Christ, the Lord of glory" (James 2:1).

18. What other evidence, in addition to the contemporary historical evidence of the gospels, do you have of the Lord's resurrection? Consider, for example. the change of the day of worship from the Sabbath, to which the Jews were fanatically attached, to the Christian Sunday. Can you explain Sunday, or Easter, apart from the Resurrection?

19. If you omit the Resurrection, can you account for the revolutionary change in the apostles from a sad group of cowards to dauntless missionaries who turned the world upside down? Can you account for the origin of the Christian Church, universally traced to Palestine around 30 A.D.? Can you explain the testimony of Christians throughout twenty centuries to their experience of a risen Lord?

Christ and the gift of the Holy Spirit

Passages: John 16:1—15, Acts 2.

Purpose: To consider the return of Jesus Christ to His Father in relation to the coming of God the Holy Spirit, and the significance of these events for the Church.

Background Material: We begin this study by leaving behind for a moment the joy and triumph of the Resurrection, and returning to John's account of the Lord's last conversations with His disciples before His trial and crucifixion. The study spans the period from that time to after Christ's ascension.

In John 14—16, Jesus talks with His sad and dispirited disciples. The Man who has loved and cared for them is preparing to leave them—not only to great personal grief, but also to great persecution: the time will come when they will be killed by people thinking to do God service (16:2). Further, He is leaving them for a humiliating and terrible death they cannot understand—a death which is the first step, as it were, in His return to God the Father. "If you loved me, you would have rejoiced, because I go to the Father (14:28)."

Associated with Christ's departure is His promise to His distressed disciples of Another like Himself—a Guide, Helper, Comforter, and Advocate—who is to be theirs in a new way and who is to remain with them.

This Spirit of grace and holiness was promised by God centuries before in such passages as Ezekiel 1:19, 20 and 36:25—29. He is given in the new covenant of Jeremiah 31:31—33 and 32:38—40. Jesus is the surety of this new covenant (Hebrews 7:22) and its mediator (Hebrews 9:15, 16)—a covenant that was bought in death, the death of the Cross.

Leader's Preparation:

1. Read John 14—16 and Luke 2, asking the Spirit of God for understanding.
2. Pray for this session and for every one who will attend it.
3. Ask God for a new realization of the person and work and love of the Holy Spirit. Remember that in condescending to live and work in, with, and through us—He being God—He shows a love no less infinite than that of the Son who became flesh and died for us, or that of the Father who sought us from eternity.

Possible Approaches:

1. Have the group reread John 16:1—15 silently. (A first reading should take place *before* they meet for study, and should include all of John 14, 15, and 16 if possible.)
2. Before you begin, set the stage for consideration of specific verses (in the following questions) along the line of the Background Material.
3. There is a wealth of subject matter in these scriptures; try to limit the group's discussion to the subject at hand: Christ and the Holy Spirit.

Discussion Questions:

1. Why does Jesus Christ say it is expedient—or to the disciples' advantage—for Him to go away?
2. In John 16:7, a negative conceals the following affirmative statement: If I go, the Comforter or Strengthener *will come.* What is implied here about the Spirit's freedom of will in His activity on our behalf?
3. Verse 7 contains another affirmation: "If I go, I will *send* him to you." Who also was sent, and at the same time, came voluntarily and with delight to do the Father's will?
4. Have three individuals in the group read John 14:16, 14:26, and 15:26. Who will send the Spirit? Since all three persons of the Godhead are involved in His giving, sending, and proceeding, what attitude should we have toward the authoritativeness of the Spirit's coming and mission? Might it be said that if we sin against the Holy Spirit, we sin against all the authority, all the love of the Trinity?
5. In John 14:16, the Spirit is given as a free gift—for our receiving, but not of our achieving. What other gift is like the gift of the Spirit in this respect? How are these gifts to be received?
6. Have someone read John 16:26, 27. Why did Christ say He would not pray to the Father for us? Since Christ does not need to intercede for us because the Father already loves us, can we conclude that God's love is the source rather than the result of the atonement? See John 3:16, 1 John 4:7—10.
7. Compare John 14:16. Why does God the Son ask the Father for the gift of the Spirit for us? Notice the time of Jesus' prayer: upon His undertaking to do the Father's supreme will for Him, that is, offer Himself up for us. Note also the time of God's pouring out of the Spirit in answer to Christ's prayer, that is, after His ascension and glorification (Acts 2).
8. In John 16:8—11, what do we learn about the

Advocate's role in pleading the cause of Christ in the world?

(a) Verse 9: As He convicts men of sin, what is sin shown to be? Do we who claim to know Christ live, in some respects, lives of practical atheism?
(b) Verse 10: What did Christ's resurrection and acceptance with the Father prove about Him?
(c) Verse 11: How does the death of Christ foreshadow judgment to come? If sin could go unjudged by God, would He have permitted the Son of His love to suffer and die for our sins? The Cross shows the utter impossibility of sin being overlooked.

9. What functions of the Spirit of truth are listed in verses 13 and 14? Note that the purpose of the Spirit is to glorify and exalt Christ, as the Son's purpose was to glorify and exalt the Father. "He shall take of mine and show it to you" applies especially to what was particularly Christ's to bestow—as Savior and Mediator. Through His life and death, Jesus secured from the Father the promised benefits (life, righteousness, "all things").

10. Have someone read John 14:26 again. What further function of the Spirit is described? Do you see here a guarantee of the inspiration of the Gospels? The Spirit's work to the end of the world is to bring the words of Christ to our minds and hearts, filling us with His truth and the joy of the knowledge of Him.

Suggested break for a second discussion.

11. Turn to Acts 2. If you are beginning a new session now, you should have time for two or three people to take turns reading the chapter aloud. Ask someone to summarize the facts recorded, and be prepared yourself to fill in important details, if they are omitted.

12. How did the Spirit—the Agent or Executor of the Godhead—manifest Himself on the day of Pentecost? What indicates that the Spirit imparts and controls

the exercise of the Lord's gifts to His Church? See also I Corinthians 12.

13. To what did Peter appeal authoritatively to account for the phenomena seen that day?

14. How can the Holy Spirit be said to be the Dynamic of the Church? What were some of the results of His working on the day of Pentecost? For His role in the building of the Church in the Lord, uniting us to Christ and to each other, read Ephesians 2:18—22.

15. According to the Bible, what are some of the Holy Spirit's activities in relation to individual believers? Read:

(a) Romans 8:2 and 11. The Spirit of life in Christ Jesus frees us from sin and death for a life of loving obedience to God.

(b) Romans 8:15, 16. The Holy Spirit, as the Spirit of adoption, gives us confidence that we are God's children, accepted in Christ by the Father, and able thus to commune with the Godhead.

(c) First Corinthians 2:9—12. The Spirit is our Enlightener in all God's revelation of Himself.

(d) Ephesians 1:13, 14 and 4:30. We are sealed by the Holy Spirit of promise—marked by God with the stamp of God (Himself!) as belonging to Him, and preserved by Him until we come into our promised inheritance.

16. What is to be our response to the Spirit of Christ?

(a) Galatians 5:25. We are to walk by the Spirit, living close to Him—in the awareness of His presence and subject to His control.

(b) Romans 8:26, 27. We are to find through Him communion with God and power for prayer.

(c) Ephesians 4:30. We are not to grieve Him, or hurt the God who in love is present in us.

(d) I Thessalonians 5:19. We are not to quench Him, or resist His workings as the Spirit of truth, power, purity, and grace.

(e) We are to glorify Him who is the Spirit of

glory (I Peter 4:14)—and eternal God, the high and holy God who inhabits eternity and the hearts of His own (Isaiah 57:15).

17. What is the inner and outer evidence of the Holy Spirit's work in and for us? Have someone read Galatians 5:22, 23. Note that these nine graces are spoken of as fruit, not fruits—the fruit of the Spirit or the fruit of light (Ephesians 5:9, RSV). They have one root, one source, are a unity and tend to produce unity.

(a) Love to God and man is a consequence of the love of God (I John 3:16). Our joy and peace also are rooted in Him, not people or circumstances.
(b) Inner love, joy, and peace are almost bound to be associated with patience under wrongs or in putting up with one another when relationships are difficult; in kindness or gentleness of disposition; and in active goodness in relation to others.
(c) Faithfulness, meekness or not insisting on our rights, and self-control will also characterize our behavior.

18. Read, perhaps in unison, Ephesians 3:14—19.

the risen and exalted Christ

Passages: I Corinthians 15, and selected passages from Hebrews and Revelation. See Questions.

Purpose: To consider the meaning of the resurrection of Jesus Christ from the dead, and the significance for us of His present life in glory.

Background Material: "He is not here, He has risen." So rang the angelic announcement to the group of women approaching an empty tomb, looking for Jesus' body.

"But now is Christ risen from the dead"—to become, the Apostle Paul asserts triumphantly, the first fruits of the harvest of the dead. For in Him all will be brought to life. And we have been born anew to a living hope (I Peter 1:3).

No discussion of the life of Jesus Christ would be complete without some consideration of His life today, of His present position at the right hand of God, "far above all rule and authority and power and dominion, and above every name that is named, not only in this age but also in that which is to come" (Ephesians 1:21). Yet this King of kings is the Jesus who walked this earth; He is clothed still in our humanity and bears forever the marks of His death for us. He is "the Lord our Righteousness"—our Life—ready to give and to be to us all that we need, able to save us to the uttermost.

Leader's Preparation:

1. Read I Corinthians 15 and as much of the books of Hebrews and Revelation as you can. Read them in entirety, if possible. Failing that, go through these books picking out every reference to Jesus Christ. As a minimum, look up the specific references referred to in the questions.
2. As you prepare, pray that God will give you a new vision of the Lord Jesus Christ. Faith's sight of Him is dim until we see Him, once crucified, now enthroned, and coming to reign.
3. Pray that every member of the Bible study group may enter by faith into that unseen world where Christ is central, where He appears perpetually in the presence of God for us. Pray that lives may be affected by this consideration of Him.

NOTE: Be prepared to break this study into two or three sessions if needed. Don't rush.

Discussion Questions:

1. Ask someone to read I Corinthians 15:12—19. If Christ were now dead, why would our faith be futile?
2. Read John 11:25, 26. If Christ had remained dead, how would this fact have affected His claims to deity and His power to save? If He had lied to us, deliberately or through self-deception, what would be our present attitude toward Him?
3. If we have hope in Christ for this life only—for instance, hope in Christ as a wise or good man or a glorious example—why are we "of all men most to be pitied"? Can the example, even the display of the Perfect Man on earth, save us from death? Can we

ever attain Jesus' perfections by our own attempts at imitation? Would not this sinless Man and His moral demands upon us be rather an endless rebuke and the destruction of our hope?

4. Have individuals in the group read I Corinthians 15:20—22, 47—49, and 51—58. What hope would you exchange for this? What now can be our new attitude toward physical death?

5. Ask two persons to read Ephesians 2:4—7 and Colossians 3:1—3. Why does Paul mix the past, present, and future in these verses? (See also Romans 8:29, 30 in this respect.) Is God's promised future as good as accomplished? Does it make any difference to us *now*? What affect will our identification with Christ in His resurrection have on us in our day-to-day living?

6. Ask the group to read aloud Hebrews 1:1—4, considering these verses thoughtfully. How is Christ the Revelation of God (a) in His incarnation (John 1:14, 18); (2) in His work of atonement for sin (I John 4:9, 10)? What does He reveal about God?

7. In these few verses, Christ is glimpsed in His threefold office of Prophet, Priest, and King. How is He God's Prophet? In what respect is He our Priest? How is He shown here to be King?

8. Compare Philippians 2:9—11. If we refuse to acknowledge the Lordship of Christ on earth, will we be able to refuse to do so in eternity?

9. Read Hebrews 2:14—18. Why is our High Priest especially able to help us? How is His ability and fitness to be our Savior affected by His being God and Man—by the uniting of two natures in one Person?

10. Hebrews 3:1—6. How is our confidence in Christ affected by the knowledge that He was faithful in accomplishing all the work and will of God?

11. Hebrews 4:14—16. What gives us boldness to enter the presence of God? What can we count on in Christ in addition to His *ability* to save? What has

He promised to give us at the throne of grace?

12. Hebrews 7:24—28. What does it mean to us that Christ is made our High Priest by the power of an indestructible life? Will He ever be less able to save us tomorrow than He was yesterday? What condition is implied in verse 25: "He is able continually to be saving those who are continually drawing near to God through Him . . . "? What does Christ always live to do?

13. Hebrews 7:26—28. What is the character of our High Priest? Why did we need One who is "altogether lovely"?

14. Hebrews 9:12—14. What did Christ do for us in addition to obtaining eternal redemption for us? What difference does it make to us that His sacrifice was one, not only of atonement, but also of purification? As long as man has a bad conscience, can he really begin to be good or be free to serve the living God?

15. Hebrews 10:10—18. Is Christ's sacrifice final? Is it sufficient?

16. Hebrews 10:19—23. What facts do these verses summarize beautifully?

17. Hebrews 12:1—3. What attitudes and actions underlie effective living for Christ on this earth? In the race we run, where is our gaze to be riveted—on other runners, on the track, on ourselves?

18. What specific relation does Jesus have to our faith? What was His attitude toward the shame of the cross? Why? Is joy set before us also? What difference does it make in our lives that Christ is now seated at the right hand of the throne of God? Read together Hebrews 13:20, 21.

The book of Revelation is a message from the throne of God, the unveiling of the Lord Jesus Christ in glory. After a prologue, it begins with a vision of Christ standing in the midst of the churches. Then the writer John is brought into heaven, where He sees God on the throne and a scroll sealed with seven seals that no man can open.

19. Ask someone to read Revelation 5:1—6. When John sees Christ as Sovereign and Victor, at the seat of all majesty and power, what does He see? Compare John 1:29.

20. Read Revelation 5:7—14. Why particularly is Christ deemed worthy of all praise, and of having all the future committed to His care?

21. Is the Lamb that was slain alive? Yet there are the marks and the virtue of His death in Him? Since the Lamb is to be exalted for ever and ever (verse 13), what position does the reality of redeeming love hold in God's universe?

22. Revelation 6:1, 2, 12—17. What else do we learn about the Lamb? Is He always the meek and gentle Christ? Notice it is the *wrath* of the *Lamb* that is spoken of in verse 6. Is God's view of sin also that of the Lord Jesus Christ?

23. Revelation 7:9—17. What does the washing of robes in the blood of the Lamb symbolize?

24. Consider God's relationship to His people in verses 15—17. Does a King usually dwell intimately with His people, sheltering and satisfying them with His presence? In what role is the Lamb seen? Note the description of God as Comforter. Compare Revelation 20:3, 4.

25. Revelation 11:15; and 12:9—11. How did the saints described here overcome their various severe trials? What does the blood of the Lamb stand for? In Christ's death, is there even more than cleansing from sin? What is there in the Cross that supplies the motive and power for overcoming? See II Corinthians 5:14, 15.

26. Revelation 19:5—9. How is the Lamb pictured here? Who is His bride? What does God tell us about His love for us by using this figure to describe His relationship with us? Compare Isaiah 54:5 and 62:5.

27. Revelation 19:11—16. How is Christ described here? What do we learn about His names? Where else was He called the Word of God?

28. Read Revelation 21:1 and 22—27. In his vision of the new heaven and the new earth, John again sees the Lamb. In all eternity, shall we ever cease to remember His death and its meaning for us? Compare Ephesians 2:4—7.

29. Revelation 22:3—5. Again Christ appears as the Lamb. "And they shall see His face." Compare I John 3:1—3.

Read together Revelation 22:20, 21.

for further study from InterVarsity Press

Getting to Know Jesus
Paul Steeves supplies thirty daily studies divided into sections covering Jesus' deity, lordship, love, death and resurrection. paper, $1.75

Getting to Know God
Paul Steeves presents thirty Bible studies which take up five areas of the doctrine of God: his nature, sovereignty, holiness, goodness and love. paper, $1.75

Discovering the Gospel of Mark
Jane Hollingsworth helps the student discover the teachings of Jesus in Mark through inductive Bible study principles and gives directions for leading a group discussion on Mark. paper, $1.25

Jesus the Disciple Maker
Ada Lum presents eight Bible studies for personal or group use which explore Jesus' method of training and show how we too can become disciple makers. paper, $1.25

Grow Your Christian Life
This guide directs personal or group Bible study on topics such as personal evangelism, sin, fellowship, knowing God's will and Christian marriage. Designed for daily study broken into twelve major sections. paper, $2.50

Rough Edges of the Christian Life
Here are eight studies on personal problems such as identity, lack of confidence, disobedience and depression. paper, $1.25

Jeremiah, Meet the 20th Century
James W. Sire presents twelve group studies on the book of Jeremiah, pointing up the contemporary relevance of Jeremiah's life and message. paper, $2.50

In Spirit and in Truth
William Edgar offers ten Bible studies on the nature, content, practice and place of worship. paper, $1.75

Leading Bible Discussions
James Nyquist compiles practical, field-tested (both on and off campus) suggestions for leaders in preparing, leading and evaluating Bible studies. paper, $1.25